Beyond Brave

FAITH TO STAND FIRM IN

MILITARY LIFE

A Six Week Bible Study on Galatians 5 from Planting Roots

Strength to Thrive in Military Life

Written by Andrea Plotner

BEYOND BRAVE

FAITH TO STAND FIRM IN MILITARY LIFE

Copyright © 2018 Planting Roots
ISBN-13: 978-1-7326657-0-5

Cover photo by Rachael Jernigan
Cover design by Ginger Harrington
Edited by Ginger Harrington and Liz Giertz

*Planting Roots is a nonprofit organization
encouraging military women to grow in their faith.*

Enjoy the companion devotional from Planting Roots

Free to Be Brave: Moments with God for Military Life
CreateSpace Independent Publishing Platform (November 2018)

Other Books from Authors on the Planting Roots Staff

Outrageous Olives
Andrea Plotner*: **https://thehubpwoc.net/outrageous-olives-2/***

Discipleship 101
Andrea Plotner*: **https://thehubpwoc.net/2014/09/04/new-bible-studies/***

Holy in the Moment: Simple Ways to Love God and Enjoy Your Life
Ginger Harrington, Abingdon Press (2018)

Journey of a Military Wife Series
Brenda Pace, American Bible Society (2017):
Directed: Steps of Peace
Deployed: Steps of Hope
Devoted: Steps of Love
Dedicated: Steps of Faith

Medals Above My Heart: The Rewards of Being a Military Wife
Brenda Pace and Carol McGlothlin, B & H Books, 2004

The One Year Yellow Ribbon Devotional:
Take a Stand in Prayer for Our Nation and Those Who Serve
Brenda Pace and Carol McGlothlin, Tyndale House Publishers, (2008)

Olive Drab POM-Poms
Kori Yates, Crossbooks, (2011)

Marriage Maintenance for Her: Tune Up After Time Apart
Liz Giertz, CreateSpace Independent Publishing Platform (2018)

Marriage Maintenance for Him: Tune Up After Time Apart
Liz Giertz, CreateSpace Independent Publishing Platform (2018)

When Marriage Gets Messy: Overcoming 10 Common Messes Married Couples Make
Liz Giertz, CreateSpace Independent Publishing Platform (2018)

Table of Contents

Introduction

Welcome to our Planting Roots community! Over the next six weeks, we will explore the profound freedom that comes with faith in Christ. In Christ, we are free from false ideas, free from guilt and shame, and free from the lie that we must accomplish certain works to earn God's favor. Better yet, in Christ we are free to give and grow and walk with God. Our freedom in Christ makes us able to stand firm in the challenges of military life.

Freedom is worth fighting for--and it is a fight! As military women, this is a reality for us. Worldly oppression is real. Dictators and tyrants are real. Political distraction, drowsiness and naivete are real, too. These things lead to bondage if we are not alert, trained, tactical, and vigilant.

Spiritual freedom is worth the fight.

The fight for spiritual freedom is not just one-time warfare but a daily battle (Ephesians 6). Spiritual oppression is real. Spiritual dictators and tyrants are real. False teaching about faith is real (many false teachers are sincere but sincerely wrong). Spiritual distraction, drowsiness, and naiveté are also real. And these things lead to spiritual bondage if we are not vigilant, alert, trained, and tactical. This is what Galatians 5 is all about.

I remember the moment I moved from believing in God intellectually to knowing him personally (see appendix on how to accept Christ as Lord). Oh, the sweetness, the freedom, the lightness, the joy, the power, and the peace that comes from walking with God, regardless of circumstances! This same sweetness has sustained me through many military training cycles, deployments, losses, griefs, and sorrows. I can't imagine *life* without the hope of Christ, but I really can't imagine *military life* without the hope of Christ.

We study God's Word to remember what's true and reinforce our hope. James 1:25 says, "But the one who looks into the perfect law, the law of liberty, and perseveres, being no hearer who forgets but a doer who acts, he will be blessed in his doing."

Why study just one chapter of the Bible?

- Galatians 5 is Paul's practical, tactical, how-to fight-for-freedom summary statement. Feel free to read or listen to the entire chapter (or book) in advance of this study.

- Learning to study the Bible verse-by-verse (2 Timothy 3:16-17) is highly beneficial. You will be amazed at the wisdom and strength mined from a single sentence of God's Word.

- Bible Memory: Challenge yourself to memorize Galatians 5 over a six-week period. Our homework will help you learn and review. In the six weeks of our study, you will have an entire chapter of the Bible memorized. Together we can do this--so give it a try!

How This Study Works

Whether doing this study on your own or as part of a group, you will get the chance to look at some big ideas in the Bible that will impact your faith walk. If you are leading a group, check out the Facilitator's Guide in the Appendix with suggestions about structuring class time. Each week has one main lesson, reflection questions, and five days of homework to help you dig in on your own. All you need for this study is a Bible, blank notebook, and a few precious minutes each day.

Periodically, you will find a sidebar with extra information that will enable you to do more research on a topic. It's important to understand the context of what you're reading so you can see things from the perspective of the original readers.

Homework involves looking up and meditating on key words used other places in the Bible. This allows Scripture (another word for the Bible) to speak for itself while broadening and deepening our understanding of basic Bible truths. In other words, like a plant deeply rooted, we will grow up and out, maturing in our faith in Christ. Plus, the repetition will make memorization easier.

Join us in this quest to armor up, grow up and stand firm in the good fight of faith.

Free from False Ideas

Week One: Free From False Ideas

Galatians 5:1

Key Truth:
I can be brave because Christ frees me from false ideas, pursuits and priorities.

1. **Warm Up Question to Discuss or Journal:** What are some situations in life that call for bravery?
2. **Wading In:** Read Galatians 5 aloud for context. This lesson will focus on Galatians 5:1.
3. **Read & Respond:** Read the lesson below, in sections or as a whole, underlining interesting concepts.

Ideas have implications. What we believe affects how we think and act. Actions flow out of attitudes. Even as Christians, false ideas can creep in and affect our faith. This week we're talking about how false ideas and false teachers can impact our thinking.

The Good Fight for Freedom

In the military, we understand the fight for freedom. There's a battle for liberty in the spiritual realm of life as well as the physical. Some battles are obvious while others are hard to recognize. This vital struggle for freedom is the focus of Galatians 5.

My Army friend Caroline jokes that in military circles, if you show up to an event, you're usually put in charge. Military communities need volunteers. As a Christian, I'm always happy to "do my part" and pitch in. Somewhere along the line, however, I began living for my own self-importance and coveting these leadership roles. When we moved to a small town as part of an ROTC assignment, I had a rude awakening. It took more than just a beating heart to be asked to join the inner circle of civilian organizations. I felt anxious and rejected. Inwardly, I was looking to exalt my reputation, not Christ's.

I thank God for faithful friends who asked penetrating questions, helping me get to the heart of my struggle. I've found great relief in confessing my striving to God. It's taken bravery to find my identity in Christ's performance rather than mine (replacing false ideas). It's taken bravery to promote Christ rather than pursue worldly promotions (replacing false pursuits).

For freedom Christ has set us free; stand firm therefore, and do not submit again to a yoke of slavery (Galatians 5:1).

Who are the Galatians?

Ancient Galatia was in modern-day Turkey. We might think of the Galatian church as a mix of believers of various backgrounds. Some were Messianic Jews, following Christ as the long-awaited Messiah. Struggling against the desire to revert to what was familiar (following rules and regulations such as circumcision as a means of salvation), the Galatian Jews became slaves to the law again. At the same time, Galatian Gentiles (non-Jews) wanted to blend Christianity with immoral living, making them slaves to sin. Both, Paul argues, are false and lead to bondage.

Who is Paul?

Paul is the author of the letter to the Galatians and one of the most unlikely heroes of Christianity. His story begins as a self-appointed assassin, a Jewish zealot hunting and killing Christians.

Why? The Jewish people waited hundreds of years for the birth of a savior. Jesus was, and is, the promised Savior, called the Messiah, but not all Jews were or are convinced (especially Paul), despite overwhelming evidence to the contrary.

With the finest education and a spotless track record, Paul had many reasons to believe he was doing it all right before God--think Army Ranger or the equivalent. According to Philippians 3:5-6, Paul was "circumcised on the eighth day, of the people of Israel, of the tribe of Benjamin, a Hebrew of Hebrews; as to the law, a Pharisee; as to zeal, a persecutor of the church; as to righteousness under the law, blameless." Paul clearly understood what it meant to be a slave to the law. It wasn't until his miraculous encounter with Christ that he could say, "But whatever gain I had, I counted as loss for the sake of Christ." (Philippians 3:7). Read Acts 9 to learn more about this exciting story.

A Man on a Mission

It then becomes Paul's mission--literally--to preach faith in Christ alone to the Roman world.

Have you ever had (or wanted) a friend who would just pull you aside and tell you you're being stupid, in this case spiritually stupid? I have. When I was a student, I made a series of bad decisions. One of my friends was caring but direct in calling out my unwise actions.

Paul is that friend.

He knew from painful personal experience the false pursuit of righteousness apart from Christ--he had murdered for what he thought to be falsehood! Paul writes to Christians he knows and loves to tell them (in *very* plain language, as you will see) they are getting off track, being led astray by people who have the wrong idea.

Slave or Free?

Remember the Galatians were Christ followers. They wanted to please God but were "trying so hard" they began adding to Christ's finished work on the cross with man-made rules. Living in confusing times, the Galatians were influenced by false and persuasive teachers, forgetting what they had been taught. We also live in a world with many competing voices:

- We hear our own inner voice--What are we meditating on? (Philippians 4)
- We hear society's voice--Does society always have our best interest in mind? (Romans 12:2)
- We hear voices of authority--How can we tell if they are leading us in truth? (1 Thessalonians 5:21-23)

What steals your smile? Is there an area of life where you have gotten tripped up, entangled, or off track? Do you have the nagging idea or is someone telling you that Christ alone just isn't...*enough*? How could standing firm in the truth make a difference? Stick around as we discover the all-encompassing freedom we have in Christ. Understanding God's freedom will empower us to stay on track, stand firm in faith, and--like Paul--boldly stand up against falsehood.

Jesus saves. Self-righteousness enslaves.

Let's Review

- Discuss or journal: What struck you as interesting or important in today's lesson? Why?
- According to Galatians 5:1, for what reason has Christ set us free?
- Who is the author of Galatians? How would you characterize him?

Let's Reflect

- What are you hoping to gain from this Bible study?
- In what ways is it hard to accept that Jesus is enough for life, death, and everything in between?
- What steals your smile? Is there something competing for God's joy and freedom in your life?

Let's Pray

Complete the prayer starter below.

God, thank you for the freedom Christ died to accomplish. Please help me be brave in the area of... Amen.

Let's Play

Galatia was a region in modern-day Turkey. Consider trying a recipe for Turkish Meatballs this week.

Homework

Week One: Day One

Key Truth:

I can be brave because Christ frees me from the slavery of false ideas, pursuits and priorities.

The homework for this study will help you learn to study the Bible on your own. Here's how:

1. **Read** and repeat the Bible verse as a means of memorization. You will see this verse repeated daily in order to help memorize the verse..
2. **Meditate** on the key word of the day, taken from the Bible verse.
3. **Look up** the other Bible verses listed (cross references) that shed light on the key word, its meaning, and its context.
4. **Journal** your responses as a means of talking with God. Reflection accelerates understanding and insight. I like to use a simple spiral bound notebook. You can also search "bullet journal" or "Bible journaling" for creative ideas.

Read & Repeat: "For freedom Christ has set us free" (Galatians 5:1a).

Key Word: Christ

Look Up: Luke 4:16-22 and John 20:30-31

Reflect: What makes Jesus able to free those who trust in him?

What places deep within your soul desire freedom? Do you trust God to make you brave and free in these areas of your life? Why or why not?

What are some ways (other than God) you seek freedom in those areas of your life?

Week One: Day Two

Read & Repeat: "For freedom Christ has set us free" (Galatians 5:1a).

Key Word: Freedom

Look Up: 2 Corinthians 3:17-18 and James 1:25

Reflect: What do you learn about the freedom of Christ?

How would your perspective change if you focused on God and his glory?

What is one thing you can do to be "a doer who acts," not a "hearer who forgets?" How can you stand firm in God's Word?

Week One: Day Three

Read & Repeat: "For freedom Christ has set us free; stand firm therefore, and do not submit again to a yoke of slavery" (Galatians 5:1).
Key Word: Slavery
Look Up: Romans 8:12-17
Reflect: How do these verses describe spiritual slavery?

Are there areas of your life where you feel like a slave?

How can the truth that you are God's daughter nurture courage in your life? What is one way you can stand firm in this vital truth?

Week One: Day Four

Read & Repeat: "For freedom Christ has set us free; stand firm therefore, and do not submit again to a yoke of slavery" (Galatians 5:1).
Key Word: Yoke/Burden
Look Up: Acts 15:10-11 and Matthew 11:29
Reflect: How would you contrast the world's yoke vs. Christ's?

Write down the ways you have tried to earn God's favor. What role has fear played in your efforts to please God?

When have you felt burdened, unable to continue?

Week One: Day Five

Read & Repeat: "For freedom Christ has set us free; stand firm therefore, and do not submit again to a yoke of slavery" (Galatians 5:1).

Key Phrase: Stand Firm

Look Up: Ephesians 6:10-18, 2 Thessalonians 2:13-17, and James 1:25

Reflect: What are we to stand firm, or persevere, in doing?

In what areas of your life is God telling you to stand firm?

What is one thing you can do to stand firm in each of those areas?

Free from Spiritual Striving

Week Two: Free From Spiritual Striving

Galatians 5:2-6

Key Truth:

I can be brave because God judges me on Christ's merits and empowers me by grace.

1. **Warm Up Question:** What are some situations in life that call for bravery?
2. **Wading In:** Read Galatians 5 aloud for context. This lesson will focus on Galatians 5:2-6.
3. **Read & Respond:** Read the lesson below, in sections or as a whole, underlining interesting concepts.

Imagine living in a political system where you are considered a criminal if you break even one law...speeding, jaywalking, throwing out an old tenant's junk mail. What a terrifying thought! In the military, there are standards about running shoes that separate the toes (toe sneakers), regulation writing pens and using indecent language (fill in the blank).

Many people try to earn their way to God by "being a good person," but by whose definition?

Remember our plain-spoken friend Paul (the author of Galatians) who is going to tell us when we are getting off track spiritually? We will be memorizing these verses this week. For now, just read and soak in the content. Here's what he says about our trying to "add" to Christ's finished work:

> *I, Paul, say to you that if you accept circumcision, Christ will be of no advantage to you. I testify again to every man who accepts circumcision that he is obligated to keep the whole law. You are severed from Christ, you who would be justified by the law; you have fallen away from grace. For through the Spirit, by faith, we ourselves eagerly wait for the hope of righteousness. For in Christ Jesus neither circumcision nor uncircumcision counts for anything, but only faith working through love. (Galatians 5:2-6)*

Obligated to Keep the Whole Law

Back to our starting illustration, if we are trying to earn our own way to God, and his standard is perfection, then we will fail if we break even one law. That would be overwhelming, wouldn't it?

If we no longer live according to the law as the Jews did in the Old Testament, how *do* we please God?

The answer is simple yet profound. We live *by faith* as we believe that God judges us on Christ's record, not our own. God infuses our faith with his grace, a blessed gift.

Amazing Grace

What is grace? It sounds like a soft, churchy, fluffy kind of word. But it's not. It might just be the meatiest, weightiest, most profound, most beautiful concept (doctrine) in the entire Bible.

Grace is the full power and provision of God extended to us, now and forever. We are *forever* perfect in God's eyes because Jesus lived a perfect life in our place. This truth is our source of bravery because we are *now* empowered to live lives that please him via the Holy Spirit, who dwells within. I especially love the description of grace found in Titus 2 (one of my favorite passages both because it's written to women and because it's such a full picture of Christ):

> *For the grace of God has appeared, bringing salvation for all people, training us to renounce ungodliness and worldly passions, and to live self-controlled, upright, and godly lives in the present age, waiting for our blessed hope, the appearing of the glory of our great God and Savior Jesus Christ, who gave himself for us to redeem us from all lawlessness and to purify for himself a people for his own possession who are zealous for good works.* (Titus 2:11-14)

Grace. Think of a graceful ballerina. She is beautiful, yes, but also strong, skilled, controlled, and poised. My friend Kristin is a Navy veteran who is learning more about grace in an unusual way.

Kristin's Ballet Story

> *I bleed Navy blue and gold. As a parent volunteer, I became the steely-eyed, military-voiced manager during performances by my daughter's ballet society. Nobody mistook me for one of the elegant dancers. Ever. Recently, the Lord challenged me to move from my ooh-rah posture to be brave and enroll in a beginner classical ballet class. Me? A salty Navy vet?! I am just learning about ballet grace – strength under control. I have long practiced military grace – strength under control. And I'm discovering the power of Christian grace which is God's strength and control moving through me.*

Called to Wait

Though we're not all called to be dancers, we *are* called to be "waiters." Remember Galatians 5:5 which says, "For through the Spirit, by faith, we ourselves eagerly wait for the hope of righteousness." Think of the attentive waiter who looks outward with a heart ready to serve and bless. Faith is waiting eagerly upon unseen hope. Hebrews 11:1 says it this way: "Now faith is the assurance of things hoped for, the conviction of things not seen." Is your faith in God's promises characterized by faith, hope, and eagerness? If not, seize the day and let God's truth fuel your faith and courage.

If grace is so...*amazing*, why would anyone try to do anything apart from God? Impatience and independence come to mind. "Do by self" my 2-year-old used to say (sometimes wisely, sometimes not). One major reason for self-sufficiency is fear and independence. Trusting God means trading "control" or man-made outcomes for confidence in Christ, who doesn't work on our timeline. Waiting with faith can be hard to relinquish control and independence.

Faith Works Through Love Rather than Obligation

What do I do with my freedom? Galatians 5:6 says "For in Christ Jesus neither circumcision nor uncircumcision counts for anything, but only faith working through love."

Why are we talking about circumcision? If you need a reminder, go back to the study box in Week 1. Really, circumcision (or not) was a dividing issue of the time. The legalists had faith motivated by rules rather than relationship. What is "faith working through love?" You can have faith without love, and you can have love without faith. God's way has both pedaling in tandem. Secure in God's love, we are free to obey him without fear of punishment.

Have you heard people say they feel guilty when they have failed to go to church or read their Bible regularly? God's doesn't desire for his people to live in condemnation for past mistakes and sins. Freedom means we are free from past guilt (Revelation 12:10). Free from worldly regret (2 Corinthians 7:10). Free to leave sin behind (Galatians 5:16-21). Free to be grace-full. Through the work of Christ, we are free to be brave!

Jesus is more than enough.

Let's Review

- What struck you as interesting or intriguing in today's lesson?
- Based on Galatians 5:2-6, by what standard are we justified or made right in God's eyes?
- List everything you learn about Christ in Galatians 5:2-6.
- In Galatians 5:2-6, who empowers our faith? How are we to exercise our faith?
- Looking at all the verses referenced in today's lesson, what's so amazing about grace?

Let's Reflect

- In what areas do you worry about earning God's approval?
- How can walking in greater spiritual freedom help you walk in greater love?
- Using a mind map (example below), list things in which people often seek value or comfort apart from God. An example has been started below. Feel free to personalize your answers, using the mind map as a visual and creative way to pray and talk to God.

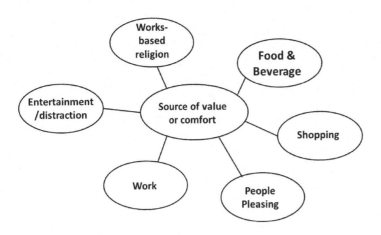

Let's Pray

God, please show me ways in which I am tempted to earn my way to You. Help me trust in you rather than my self-effort. Fill me with Your Spirit so I can be grace-full. I want to "wait" eagerly for the hope of Christ alone. Amen.

Let's Play

Turkish people are known for their warm, simple hospitality, and Turkish *chai* (black tea served with two lumps of sugar) is a staple in every home. As a way of exercising faith through love, consider inviting someone to tea this week and ask God's Spirit to help you listen well.

Homework

Week Two: Day One

Key Truth:

I can be brave because God judges me on Christ's merits and gives me grace.

 This week's homework involves memorizing five Bible verses...one for each day! Start by asking God to help you hide his Word in your heart. Two tips that work really well for me are 1) playing the chapter aloud on my phone while I'm driving and 2) reading the key verse right before I go to bed at night. At a minimum, you'll find that when someone talks about Galatians, you will have an immediate reference point in your head. The Spirit can help you be brave to work on Scripture memory!

Week Two: Day One

Read & Repeat: "Look: I, Paul, say to you that if you accept circumcision, Christ will be of no advantage to you" (Galatians 5:2).
Key Word: Circumcision
Look Up: Galatians 2:3-5
Reflect: In what way is Paul's argument against mandatory circumcision an example of faith working through love?

When do you feel pressure to comply with a "Christian" tradition that is not mandated by God?

What are some ways you can model faith working through love rather than traditions?

Week Two: Day Two

Read & Repeat: "I testify again to every man who accepts circumcision that he is obligated to keep the whole law" (Galatians 5:3).
Key Phrase: Obligated to Keep the Whole Law
Look Up: Acts 15
Reflect: What's happening in Acts 15?

In what areas of your life do you strive for perfection? What kinds of fears lurk behind our desire for perfection?

What does it feel like to realize that Jesus lived a perfect life and transferred his perfect record to you?

Week Two: Day Three

Read & Repeat: "You are severed from Christ, you who would be justified by the law; you have fallen away from grace" (Galatians 5:4).
Key Phrase: Grace
Look Up: John 1:14, Romans 5:1-2, and 1 Peter 5:12
Reflect: Name the ways God has shown you grace.

How would your perspective toward others change if you remembered the grace God gave you?

In what areas of your life do you need to stand firm in God's grace?

Week Two: Day Four

Read & Repeat: "For through the Spirit, by faith, we ourselves eagerly wait for the hope of righteousness" (Galatians 5:5).

Key Word: Hope

Look Up: Titus 2:11-14

Reflect: What exactly are Christians eagerly waiting and hoping for?

In what types of things or people do you place your hope?

When was the last time you "waited expectantly" for something?

Week Two: Day Five

Read & Repeat: "For in Christ Jesus neither circumcision nor uncircumcision counts for anything, but only faith working through love" (Galatians 5:6).
Key Phrase: Faith Working Through Love
Look Up: Hebrews 11 and 1 Thessalonians 1:1-5
Reflect: List 5 things you learn about faith from Hebrews 11.

1.

2.

3.

4.

5.

In 1 Thessalonians 1:1-5, why do you think faith and love are mentioned together?

What are some ways faith can work through love?

In what ways have you seen faith without love?

Free from Spiritual Uncertainty

Free From Spiritual Uncertainty

Galatians 5:7-12

Key Truth:

I can be brave because I know God's voice of truth.

1. **Warm Up Question:** Can you think of a time you experienced a hindrance in your spiritual life?
2. **Wading In:** Read Galatians 5 aloud for context. This lesson will focus on Galatians 5:7-12.
3. **Read & Respond:** Read the lesson below, in sections or as a whole, underlining interesting bits.

In military terms, a hindrance is a tactical obstacle to slow down the enemy. Combat engineers, for example, might blow up a road to prevent vehicles from moving forward. For an actual runner, a hindrance might be an external obstacle (like a roadblock) or internal impediment (such as an injury).

The Galatian Christians, as we have been discussing for the past two weeks, were hindered spiritually by false teaching and false teachers. And although false teachers may or may not deliberately lead people astray, the Bible says all falsehood ultimately stems from spiritual forces of evil. Our job is to recognize the fight and armor up daily!

But the Galatians were slipping into old patterns, and this Scripture is Paul's last-ditch effort to rescue them from deadly error:

> *You were running well. Who hindered you from obeying the truth? This persuasion is not from him who calls you. A little leaven leavens the whole lump. I have confidence in the Lord that you will take no other view, and the one who is troubling you will bear the penalty, whoever he is. But if I, brothers, still preach circumcision, why am I still being persecuted? In that case the offense of the cross has been removed. I wish those who unsettle you would emasculate themselves!* (Galatians 5:7-12)

How to Run Well

Paul says the Galatian Christians had been running well, so let's consider how to run well in Christ.

1. **Eye on the Prize:** Although a hindrance may slow you down, it is essential to stay on track and keep your eye on the prize. Paul says this in Philippians 3:12-16:

   Not that I have already obtained this or am already perfect, but I press on to make it my own, because Christ Jesus has made me his own. Brothers, I do not consider that I have made it my own. But one thing I do: forgetting what lies behind and straining forward to what lies ahead, I press on toward the goal for the **prize of the upward call of God in Christ Jesus.** *Let those of us who are mature think this way, and if in anything you think otherwise, God will reveal that also to you. Only let us hold true to what we have attained.* (emphasis added)

2. **Constant Practice:** Military members understand the value of training. Consistent discipline--obeying the truth--is a mark of maturity. When we let our spiritual attention wane, we are more susceptible to falsehood. Listen to Hebrews 5:14, speaking about the discernment that comes from *regularly* feasting on God's Word: *But solid food is for the mature, for those who have their powers of discernment trained by constant practice to distinguish good from evil.*

3. **Listen to the Right Coach or Drill Sergeant:** Paul asks the Galatians, "Who hindered you from obeying the truth? This persuasion is not from him who calls you." Think of all the viral advice on the internet on the best diet for athletes. Some recommend low carb, some high carb, some low fat, some high fat.... Eternity is not a trial-and-error proposition! Here's what Jesus says in John 10:27-28: *My sheep hear my voice, and I know them, and they follow me. I give them eternal life, and they will never perish, and no one will snatch them out of my hand.*

A Little Leaven

When Paul says, "a little leaven leavens the whole lump," he is essentially saying that even bad ideas can go viral. If we are not discerning, it's easy to get caught up in lies and falsehood. We can discern the truth with God's Word!

Let's consider one lie many women believe: My body image determines my worth. This ugly message is reinforced again and again. We're talking *a lot* of leaven in this case, and even many faith-full women are not immune. In Paul's day the lie was Christ + circumcision = salvation. What are some of the false add-ons to faith today?

The Offense of the Cross

Paul concludes by talking about "the offense of the cross." There are reasons we sometimes feel awkward or fearful in talking to others about our faith because the message is not "politically correct". Christianity pivots around the fact you can't save yourself. The Bible says people do have a sin nature, there really was a worldwide flood, and Noah's Ark is not a fairy tale. The Bible talks about right and wrong, good and evil, truth and lies. Jesus himself says he is the only way to heaven (John 14:6). Yes, our faith is an offense to a relativistic culture. 2 Corinthians 2:16 (NIV) reminds us of this truth: *To the one we are an aroma that brings death; to the other, an aroma that brings life.*

Spiritual Certainty

Spiritual certainty is grounded in identity, knowing you are a follower of a very Good Shepherd. The runner sees herself as an athlete in training. Like the runner, soldier, or sheep, our identity with Christ shapes our loyalty, our activity, and our hope. Truth shields us from falsehood. The certainty of truth makes us brave!

In the same way you can be married ("faith") and spend lots or little time with your husband ("works"), we choose to spend time with Christ. But it's in the spending time together that we share our lives, grow together, and begin to operate as one. Time with Christ makes us more certain of his unconditional love.

Christian baptism involves identifying outwardly with Christ like a marriage service. *We were buried therefore with him by baptism into death, in order that, just as Christ was raised from the dead by the glory of the Father, we too might walk in newness of life* (Romans 6:4).

Was there a time you were running well spiritually? When? Have you gotten derailed? Paul is like a parent trying to protect his children from bad influences. Will you take your stand?

Spiritual certainty grounds our worth in Christ.

Let's Review

- What caught your attention as you read today's lesson? Why?
- How does Paul define "running well" in Galatians 5:7?
- How seriously does Paul take false teaching and false teachers? Why? Give examples.
- In what ways is the "offense" of Christianity or the cross obvious in modern culture?
- How does identifying with Christ impact our spiritual certainty?

Let's Reflect

- Have you ever run a race or trained athletically? How are you running spiritually?
- What does the fight for truth look like in your heart and life?
- What are some practical ways you can spend time with Christ?

Let's Pray

God, thank you for the strong reminder that I need to be on guard against spiritual lies and false teachers. Please help me stand firm in truth and recognize the voice of my Good Shepherd, Jesus. Amen.

Let's Play: Try this popular Greek bread, a two-ingredient Pita Bread: 1 cup self-rising flour and 1 cup Greek yogurt. Roll into discs and cook on a hot griddle, turning once. Salt to taste and eat plain or with hummus!

Homework

Week Three: Day One

Key Truth:

I can be brave because I know God's voice of truth.

 How's the memory work going? I remember trying to memorize the first chapter of James. One of my friends despairingly said, "I only memorized three verses this week!" That's not cause for despair! Here's another memory tip that should be easy with this week's passage, Galatians 5:7-12. Using your blank notebook, break the section down into an outline that speaks to you:

    I.   Run
   II. Leaven
  III. Call
  IV. Cross
   V. Papa Bear's Insult

Read & Repeat: "You were running well. Who hindered you from obeying the truth?" (Galatians 5:7).
Key Word: Run
Look Up: Hebrews 12:1-2 and Psalm 119:32
Reflect: In what areas of your life do you need to run well?

What fears play a role in the thoughts, attitudes, choices, or behaviors that hinder you?

When you look at your race today, how can you keep your eyes on God rather than the obstacles?

Week Three: Day Two

Read & Repeat: "This persuasion is not from him who calls you" (Galatians 5:8).
Key Phrase: Him Who Calls You
Look Up: Matthew 4:18-22, Matthew 5, and Matthew 22:1-14
Reflect: What are some ways Christ calls you to follow him?

Write a prayer of gratitude to God for calling you to faith.

Write out 3 specific ways to follow Christ in your life this week.

Week Three: Day Three

Read & Repeat: "A little leaven leavens the whole lump. I have confidence in the Lord that you will take no other view, and the one who is troubling you will bear the penalty, whoever he is" (Galatians 5:9-10).

Key Phrase: One Who Is Troubling You

Look Up: 1 John 2:4, Romans 6:17, and John 8:31

Reflect: What do you learn about the Bible's view of false teachers in these passages?

Where can you see false teachers in our world today? What messages do they proclaim? How do they capitalize on fear to manipulate people?

What personal, religious, or societal messages have you believed that you now realize do not align with God's truth? How is the truth set you free?

Week Three: Day Four

Read & Repeat: "But if I, brothers, still preach circumcision, why am I still being persecuted? In that case the offense of the cross has been removed" (Galatians 5:11).

Key word: Cross

Look up: Romans 9:33 and 1 Corinthians 1:23

Reflect: In what ways has God used the cross to make you certain of his love?

Before you became a Christian, what was your impression of the cross?

How has your perspective changed?

Week Three: Day Five

Read & Repeat: "I wish those who unsettle you would emasculate themselves!" (Galatians 5:12).

Key Words: Agitators; False Teachers

Look Up: Romans 2:8 and Galatians 2:4

Reflect: How would you advise someone you care about to resist falsehood and stand firm in truth?

What are some ways you can protect yourself and your family from lies?

Do you have a situation or relationship that needs to experience God's truth? What could you say to bravely share the truth with love?

Free
to
Live
and
Love

Week Four: Free to Live and Love

Galatians 5:13-15

Key Truth:
I can be brave because God frees me from self-preservation.

1. **Warm Up Question:** Can you think of a time someone loved you generously and sacrificially?
2. **Wading In:** Read Galatians 5 aloud for context. This lesson will focus on Galatians 5:13-15.
3. **Read & Respond:** Read the lesson below, in sections or as a whole, underlining interesting concepts.

Historic Freedom Fails

The Golden Calf (Exodus 32)

Shortly after deliverance (and freedom!) from Egyptian slavery, Moses went up Mt. Sinai to receive God's message for His people. Impatient with Moses' delay, the people "made their own God" by melting gold and forming it into a idol (idle?) statue. Though called to God's freedom, they returned to man-made bondage.

The French Revolution

Revolting against the authority of both God (the church) and men (the monarchy), the French people overthrew the government in one of the most brutal and bloody periods in human history. Seeking "Liberty, Equality, and Fraternity" apart from God, the French tragically found none, and were soon enslaved by a new emperor.

There's a new book series out there on healthy eating called *Eat This, Not That!* helping people make good food choices among many options. That's the direction Paul is headed in our next three verses in Galatians 5. Mid-chapter, Paul moves from telling us what *not* to do with our freedom to what *to* do (love one another):

For you were called to freedom, brothers. Only do not use your freedom as an opportunity for the flesh, but through love serve one another. For the whole law is fulfilled in one word: "You shall love your neighbor as yourself." But if you bite and devour one another, watch out that you are not consumed by one another. (Galatians 5:13-15)

Called to Freedom

I love the variety of military life, but have suffered major bouts of anxiety surrounding moves, deployments, and the inevitable periods of waiting to find out about (fill in the blank). Anxiety is a form of significant emotional bondage. Hard on the heels of my anxiety is often anger, the spoiled fruit of my fearful heart. Anger holds emotions captive, causing regret for the wounds my words inflict on those I love. Regret enslaves our hearts as well. God, through His Word, calls me out of sin's captivity and into freedom.

What God Says About Anxiety:

You keep him in perfect peace whose mind is stayed on you, because he trusts in you (Isaiah 26:3).

What God Says About Anger:

> *He who is slow to anger is better than a warrior,*
> *and he who controls his temper is greater than one who captures a city* (Proverbs 16:32 BSB).

What God Says About Regret:

> *Godly sorrow brings repentance that leads to salvation and leaves no regret,*
> *but worldly sorrow brings death* (2 Corinthians 7:10 NIV).

Here's the thing: Spiritual bondage makes it hard to focus on God and others. I am self-absorbed. Spiritual captivity is an "all-about-me" proposition. Self-preservation, fear of not getting my needs met, doesn't leave much room for others. When I accept the liberty Christ offers, I find freedom which enables me to live for God, to love God, to live beyond myself. Knowing my needs are met in Christ makes me brave. Freedom also releases me to love, encourage and help others because my need are met in Christ.

Freedom is an Opportunity

If you have "*free time,*" you have the *freedom* to choose how to spend it. I find it quite tempting to spend time for my own pleasure or purposes if I'm not in step with the Spirit. But Paul warns us, "do not use your freedom as an opportunity for the flesh." Fear tempts many of us to pursue legalistic solutions. A religious form of bondage, legalism happens when we impose external rules and regulations so we *can't* act selfishly. God's solution is to serve one another because of love rather than rules. Paul instructs us to love God and others, calling us to relationship. Serve from a loving overflow of gratitude rather than a rule mentality. Selfish "me time" never seems to strengthen me anyway, but giving my life away for God's glory and the good of others fulfills my God-given purpose with joy.

Elliot's Commentary for English Readers says it this way, "He who loves his neighbor as himself will need no other rule. On the other hand, dissensions will be fatal, not to one party only, but to all who take part in them."[1]

Is there an area of life where you feel selfish, despite being freed to live for others? What truth will help you stand firm? This might be a good time to talk about mobile devices (chagrin). Military life makes social media a mixed bag. It's great to keep in touch long distance, but it can be easy to live "virtually" instead of living in our current "reality." It's fun to see what others are doing, but how do we feel when we compare our lives to theirs? Or what are we really saying when we post only the positive about ourselves rather than the whole picture?

Wild Animals

Paul uses graphic language to describe what we look like when we "bite and devour" one another. All of the shackles we've been discussing--Anxiety, anger, regret, legalism, and the envy of comparison are just a few of the shackles that lead to conflict when we fight to preserve ourselves. While I hate conflict, I do like getting my own way. James is instructive here. Here are two of my favorite pieces of advice in the Bible. Which one speaks to you at the moment? Why?

- *Let every person be quick to hear, slow to speak, slow to anger; for the anger of man does not produce the righteousness of God* (James 1:19-20).
- *What causes fights and quarrels among you? Don't they come from your desires that battle within you?* (James 4:1 NIV).

There is a smallness that comes from living in survival mode and needing to have my own way. Boxing us in, fear of failure, rejection, or loss become walls that limit rather than protect. By contrast, there is joy, delight, freedom, and strength that comes from walking in God's big spaces, satisfied with His Spirit and full to overflowing. This is the beyond-brave life that God desires to give us. See Psalm 118:5 for encouragement on this topic.

---

[1] http://biblehub.com/commentaries/galatians/5-13.htm

Love One Another

There are so many amazing passages in the Bible that teach us how to love others.. Here are several "one another" verses in the Bible that show us how to treat others. Fill in the chart at on the next page. If you are doing this Bible study as a group, consider using a whiteboard to fill in the chart together.

One Another Verse	How to Love & Serve One Another
Galatians 5:13	Example: Through love serve one another
Galatians 6:2	
1 Peter 1:22	
1 Peter 4:9	
Philippians 2:3-4	
Ephesians 4:32	
1 Thessalonians 3:12	
1 Thessalonians 5:11	
John 13:34-35	
Hebrews 10:24	
Romans 12:10	

Jesus said it best:

"It is more blessed to give than to receive."

(Acts 20:35)

Let's Review

- What caught your attention as you read today's lesson? Why?
- What one word sums up the entire Mosaic law and how is that possible?

Let's Reflect

- As you look at Paul's "Do This, Not That!" instructions this week, what speaks to you? Why?
- How have you experienced "Love your neighbor as yourself" in military life?
- What ways have anxiety, anger, regret, or comparison held you captive?

Let's Pray

God, give me courage to love you by doing _____ this week. Amen.

Let's Play: The Newsboys have an old-school worship song *I Am Free* (2006). Consider listening to it now. Christ has set us free to live for him in joy, in song, in wide open places. Our shackles are off!

Homework

Week Four: Day One

Key Truth:

I can be brave because God frees me from self-preservation.

 Memory Tip: Another great memory device is setting words to song. This week, try taking a simple or favorite tune and use it to memorize Galatians 5:13-15.

Read & Repeat: "For you were called to freedom, brothers. Only do not use your freedom as an opportunity for the flesh, but through love serve one another" (Galatians 5:13).
Key Word: Flesh
Look Up: Mark 14:38 and 1 John 2:15-17
Reflect: How is the flesh at war with the Spirit? What is one way you can resist the flesh, and live by the Spirit?

Write about a time (maybe even today!) when you felt your "flesh" taking over. Write a prayer inviting the Holy Spirit into your everyday moments.

In what areas of your life is your spirit willing but your flesh weak? Ask God to strengthen you with faith and courage in these areas.

Week Four: Day Two

Read & Repeat: "For you were called to freedom, brothers. Only do not use your freedom as an opportunity for the flesh, but through love serve one another" (Galatians 5:13).
Key Phrase: Serve
Look Up: Ephesians 5:21 and 1 Peter 2:16
Reflect: How do these verses inspire you to serve God and others?

Describe a time when someone served you in love. What was most meaningful to you about that experience?

Think of 3 people you can serve. What would it look like to serve them this week?

When you start to have a bad attitude about serving, how can you concentrate on God instead?

Week Four: Day Three

Read & Repeat: "For the whole law is fulfilled in one word: 'You shall love your neighbor as yourself'" (Galatians 5:14).

Key Word: Love

Look Up: Matthew 22:34-40 and Galatians 6:2

Reflect: How do *you* like to be treated?

What does the word neighbor mean to you? Make a list of some of your neighbors.

What is something unexpected you could do to show your love for someone?

Week Four: Day Four

Read & Repeat: "For the whole law is fulfilled in one word: 'You shall love your neighbor as yourself'" (Galatians 5:14).
Key Phrase: Law Fulfilled
Look Up: Matthew 22:34-40 and Romans 13:8-10
Reflect: Can you explain how love fulfills God's law?

What does unconditional love look like in your life?

List the ways Jesus fulfilled God's law.

Take a moment to thank Jesus for fulfilling the law on your behalf.

Week Four: Day Five

Read & Repeat: "But if you bite and devour one another, watch out that you are not consumed by one another" (Galatians 5:15).

Key Phrase: Bite and Devour

Look Up: James 3:14-18

Reflect: Describe a time when someone treated you unfairly. How did this situation make you feel?

Have you been able to release the person's offense to God's justice?

Is there a relationship or situation where you need to put your sharp fangs and claws away and look for God's solution?

In what ways does it take courage to be a peacemaker?

Free to Follow God's Spirit

Week Five: Free to Follow God's Spirit

Galatians 5:16-21

Key Truth:

I can be brave because God is a good leader.

1. **Warm Up:** Play the game, Two Truths and a Lie. Share three things you love or dislike about military life, but state one as the opposite. (Example: "I hate moving" would mean you enjoy moving, etc.). Try to identify which statement is the opposite for each member of the class. We will do a similar activity later to get to know more about the Spirit.
2. **Wading In:** Read Galatians 5 aloud for context. This lesson will focus on Galatians 5:16-21.
3. **Read & Respond:** Read the lesson below, in sections or as a whole, underlining interesting concepts.

A recent study of corporate CEOs identified four behaviors that set these leaders apart:

1. Decisiveness
2. Buy In
3. Reliability
4. Adaptability

In the article, Ruth Umoh observes that strong leaders "Establish everyday routines and habits to build relationships."[2] Cultivating relationship-building routines is a practical way to "love one another" without being drained or neglecting real priorities. The best leaders I've known *are* relational, not just all work.

---

[2] https://www.cnbc.com/2018/03/16/4-behaviors-that-transform-ordinary-people-into-ceos.html

What does all this talk about leadership have to do with this week's exhortation from Paul? He reminds us to walk in step with the Spirit, to follow God's good leadership, and he will transform our desires from the inside out.

> *But I say, walk by the Spirit, and you will not gratify the desires of the flesh. For the desires of the flesh are against the Spirit, and the desires of the Spirit are against the flesh, for these are opposed to each other, to keep you from doing the things you want to do. But if you are led by the Spirit, you are not under the law. Now the works of the flesh are evident: sexual immorality, impurity, sensuality, idolatry, sorcery, enmity, strife, jealousy, fits of anger, rivalries, dissensions, divisions, envy, drunkenness, orgies, and things like these. I warn you, as I warned you before, that those who do such things will not inherit the kingdom of God.* (Galatians 5:16-21)

Follow the Leader

This is the whole lesson: Follow the leader. Follow God. Walk in step, in cadence, with the Spirit.

Paul is giving us another contrast, another DO THIS, NOT THAT! What do we do? Follow the divine leader! When you are in a relationship with someone, you spend time with them. You share. You do life together. God is not your distant third cousin twice removed. He is near and dear. James 4:8 says, "Draw near to God and he will draw near to you." Let him lead you.

Get to Know the Spirit

Let's talk about the Holy Spirit. The Spirit is God's personal presence, abiding within us. I like to think of the Spirit as the oil that makes life run smoothly or the electricity that powers a lightbulb.

The Spirit is the third person of the Godhead--Father, Son and Holy Spirit (often called the Trinity, though you won't find this term in Scripture). The Holy Spirit came upon select individuals in the Old Testament, sometimes called the Age of Law, but lives within believers in our Age of Grace. This is what Jesus told his followers about the Spirit before his death and resurrection described in the New Testament:

And I will ask the Father, and he will give you another Helper, to be with you forever, even the Spirit of truth, whom the world cannot receive, because it neither sees him nor knows him. You know him, for he dwells with you and will be in you. (John 14:15-17)

In other translations of this passage, the term "Helper" is alternately described as Advocate, Comforter, Counselor, and Redeemer. What a powerful, pivotal and beautiful role! Do you regularly live with the awareness that you have an advocate within you (one who goes to bat on your behalf), a comforter (one who soothes your soul), a counselor (one with infinite wisdom who guides and advises you), and a redeemer (one who cashes in on promises and turns situations to your greatest eternal advantage)? What circumstance of your life needs the Spirit's touch right now? Trust his good leadership and he will make you brave.

The Opposites Game

Paul tells us that the desires of the Spirit are contrary to the desires of the flesh, so we are talking about appetites here (truly EAT THIS, NOT THAT). I used to discipline myself to eat veggies simply to be healthy; now I eat them because I crave them. A friend of mine had a great little saying about appetites and desires:

Discipline leads to desire.

Desire leads to delight.

We will look at the key word "desire" in this week's homework, but for now let's play what I call "The Opposites Game." Paul has given us a list of sixteen things that are contrary to the Spirit, so let's learn more about what the Spirit is like by finding their opposites.

Fill in the blanks under God's Spirit with the opposites of the words listed under Worldly Activity.

Worldly Activity	**God's Spirit**
Sexual Immorality	Holy
Impurity	
Sensuality	
Idolatry	
Sorcery	
Enmity	
Strife	
Jealousy	
Fits of Anger	
Rivalries	
Dissensions	

The Kingdom of God

Finally, Paul issues a serious warning: Choosing the flesh over the Spirit has eternal consequences. If we are seeking first the kingdom of God (Matthew 6:33), we start with walking by the spirit not the flesh.

The Spirit transforms, soothes, and guides our soul from within.

Let's Review

- What does Paul say is the result of walking in cadence with God's Spirit? With the flesh?
- What is the central--and eternal--warning to those who choose the flesh over the Spirit?

Let's Reflect

- How would you describe your walk with God? How could you live more fully in step with the Spirit?

Let's Pray: *God, thank you for providing good leadership. Please help me heed your Word! Amen.*

Let's Play: This week, express appreciation for someone you know in leadership.

Homework

Week Five: Day One

Key Truth:

I can be brave because God is a good leader.

Study Tip: Looking at the original Greek New Testament is a hands-on way to study the Bible. There are many study tools out there which help you do this. If you go to http://biblehub.com/text/galatians/5-16.htm you can see the word used for Spirit is *Pneuma,* which roughly translates *wind.* Wind, though invisible, is a powerful, guiding, God-given force. Consider using a Bible tool to dig a little deeper this week. Be brave!

Read & Repeat: "But I say, walk by the Spirit, and you will not gratify the desires of the flesh" (Galatians 5:16).
Key Word: Spirit
Look Up: Matthew 1:20, Matthew 3, and Matthew 28:19
Reflect: Make a list of what you learn about God's Spirit in the passages above.

What could it look like if you rely on the Spirit to lead you to live in freedom from the desires of your flesh? To what extent has fear triggered your flesh?

How can you rely on the leadership of the Holy Spirit today?

Week Five: Day Two

Read & Repeat: "But I say, walk by the Spirit, and you will not gratify the desires of the flesh. For the desires of the flesh are against the Spirit, and the desires of the Spirit are against the flesh, for these are opposed to each other, to keep you from doing the things you want to do" (Galatians 5:16-17).

Key Word: Walk (conduct my life)

Look Up: Romans 6:4, Romans 8:1-8, 2 Corinthians 5:7, and Ephesians 4

Reflect: In what ways has God been walking alongside you?

What are three ways you can set your mind on "the things of the Spirit?" How can this help you stand firm in life?

In what areas of your military experience do you need to walk by faith and not by sight?

Make a list of practical ways you can walk in a worthy manner in your current season of life.

Week Five: Day Three

Read & Repeat: "But if you are led by the Spirit, you are not under the law" (Ephesians 5:18).
Key Phrase: Led by the Spirit
Look Up: John 16:13, 2 Timothy 1:7, and Hebrews 2:10
Reflect: What does it mean to you to be led by the Spirit?

How have you experienced the Spirit's leadership giving you strength, wisdom, or courage?

Think of a brave person in your life who is led by the Spirit. How have you seen them stand firm in God's Word?

How can believing God has given you a spirit of power, love, and self-control ignite courage to address challenges in your life?

Week Five: Day Four

Read & Repeat: "But if you are led by the Spirit, you are not under the law" (Ephesians 5:18).
Key Phrase: Under the (Mosaic) Law
Look Up: Luke 2:22-52
Reflect: What did you learn about the law in regards to the Jewish people's everyday life before Christ?

What are some requirements Jews had to follow in Jesus's day? What does it mean to you that you are not under the law? How can this truth free you from fear of failure?

What are some ways Christians can fall into a law mentality today?

Week Five: Day Five

Read & Repeat: "Now the works of the flesh are evident: sexual immorality, impurity, sensuality, idolatry, sorcery, enmity, strife, jealousy, fits of anger, rivalries, dissensions, divisions, envy, drunkenness, orgies, and things like these. I warn you, as I warned you before, that those who do such things will not inherit the kingdom of God" (Galatians 5:19-21).

Key Phrase: Kingdom of God

Look Up: Matthew 6:33 and Matthew 13

Reflect: Review the works of the flesh. Repent of the ones you see in yourself.

These are the product of being "in the flesh." Pray that God would lead you in the Spirit instead.

As you contrast the kingdom of the world with the kingdom of God, which areas of your life reflect God's kingdom? Which reflect the world's?

What are some ways you can fearlessly advance God's kingdom on earth?

Free
to
Grow
in
God

Week Six: Free to Grow in the Spirit

Galatians 5:22-25

Key Truth:

I can be brave because God is the source of my growth.

1. **Warm Up:** Name military situations where you gained confidence with safeguards in place.
2. **Wading In:** Read Galatians 5 aloud for context. This lesson will focus on Galatians 5:22-25.
3. **Read & Respond:** Read the lesson below, in sections or as a whole, underlining interesting concepts.

We live in Idaho's huckleberry country, between Fairchild and Mountain Home Air Force Bases. Huckleberries are wild blueberries that are small but packed with flavor. Huckleberry picking is serious business because they are hand-foraged in the wild during late summer, high up in the mountains between 2,000-8,000 feet above sea level.

Paul tells us in Galatians 5 that we are like fruit trees (or berry bushes, if you like):

But the fruit of the Spirit is love, joy, peace, patience, kindness, goodness, faithfulness, gentleness, self-control; against such things there is no law. And those who belong to Christ Jesus have crucified the flesh with its passions and desires. If we live by the Spirit, let us also keep in step with the Spirit. Let us not become conceited, provoking one another, envying one another. (Galatians 5:22-25)

What kind of fruit is produced in your life? Plump, juicy fruit or fruit that's shriveled and sour? If you stop and think about it, no fruit tree or berry bush "works" to produce fruit. Fruit is a by-product of its health, wellness, and growing conditions. The same is true for us spiritually. Bible scholar David Guzik says it this way, "Fruit isn't achieved by working, but is birthed by abiding."[3]

Abiding is a beautiful, life-giving concept in the Bible, meaning to live or dwell. It's where we get the word abode, or dwelling place. Let me ask you this: How important is housing—your

---

[3] https://enduringword.com/bible-commentary/galatians-5/

abode—to you each time the military moves you? If where we live for two to three years in this life is important to us, how much more important is our spiritual home?

As we walk in step with the Spirit, God becomes our greenhouse and our gardener. The greenhouse is a place of both protection and nourishment, and God, the master gardener of our souls, nurtures us with love and mercy.

Be steadfast in these encouraging truths about abiding or dwelling with God:

- *Abide in me, and I in you. As the branch cannot bear fruit by itself, unless it abides in the vine, neither can you, unless you abide in me* (John 15:4).
- *Surely goodness and mercy shall follow me all the days of my life, and I shall dwell in the house of the Lord forever* (Psalm 23:6).
- *One thing have I asked of the Lord, that will I seek after: that I may dwell in the house of the Lord all the days of my life, to gaze upon the beauty of the Lord and to inquire in his temple* (Psalm 27:4).

We seek after God by abiding in His Word and in prayer as we listen to and talk with him. Get creative in your "walk" with God:

- Walk with friends whom you can encourage or be encouraged by.
- Walk through Bible passages as you study.
- Walk through your day mindful of Christ.

Fresh from the Vine

I've had some amazing fruit dishes--strawberry rhubarb pie, peach pie, apple pie, or a simple bowl of mixed berries with lemon curd. Fruit is a picture of the good life. People think you have to "give up all your fun" to follow God, but it's just not true!

God's wants us to thrive by walking in courage, wholeness, and peace. Let's play the opposites game again, contrasting God's fruit vs. the world's fruit. Which appeals to you? Are there areas where the flesh and the world still captivate you? Using Galatians 5:22 as your guide, consider the fruit of the spirit and identify opposing characteristics. Complete the chart on the next page.

List the Fruit of the Spirit	List the Opposite of the Fruit of the Spirit
Love	Indifference

Crucify the Flesh

Paul says that we have been crucified with Christ, including our flesh. It's easy to "play" the opposites game by filling in a chart, but much harder to resist a major temptation. The key is *confession* and *repentance*. Confession is agreeing with God about my wrongdoing (vs. justifying my actions). Repentance is turning away from wrongdoing and walking in the opposite direction. Understanding that we are free from the burden of sin empowers us to courageously face our issues and sins.

- *I have been crucified with Christ. It is no longer I who live, but Christ who lives in me. And the life I now live in the flesh I live by faith in the Son of God, who loved me and gave himself for me (Galatians 2:20).*
- *If we confess our sins, he is faithful and just to forgive us our sins and to cleanse us from all unrighteousness (I John 1:9).*
- *Repent therefore, and turn back, that your sins may be blotted out, that times of refreshing may come from the presence of the Lord (Acts 4:19-20a).*

Don't Boast About Your Blue Ribbon

Paul ends by warning us not to become conceited, provoking or envious. Why? Like the huckleberry, our fruit is extremely valuable! Here's a military way to look at this: Are you tempted with pride when you get promoted or receive an award? When things are going well in life, it's easy to forget God, confident that you've got your act together. When a friend is promoted below the zone, do you jump to jealousy or are you truly happy for them? As we experience spiritual freedom and victory, let's humbly give thanks to Jesus who makes it all possible. And unlike huckleberry foragers, let's not keep our source of our success a secret!

The Spirit gives us strength to thrive in military life.

Let's Review

- List the fruit of the Spirit and circle the one you feel you need the most.
- What are Christ-followers to do with the passions and desires of the flesh?

Let's Reflect

- What is your most significant personal take-away from this Bible study? Tell God all about it.

Let's Pray

- *God, thank you for your freedom in Christ. Help me humbly walk in step with your Spirit! Amen.*

Let's Play

- Come up with a creative way to spend time alone with God. Plan to extend your worship or meditation session one day this week, or even go berry picking with new eyes.

Homework

Week Six: Day One

Key Truth:

I can be brave because God is the source of my growth.

Although a Bible study like this one can be helpful, you don't need a lesson plan to read God's Word. We have given you tools in the back of this study to help you study on your own:

- How to Read the Bible for Personal Study
- How to Memorize Scripture
- How to Pray

Read & Repeat: "But the fruit of the Spirit is love, joy, peace, patience, kindness, goodness, faithfulness, gentleness, self-control; against such things there is no law" (Galatians 5:22-23).
Key Word: Fruit
Look Up: Matthew 7:16-20 and John 15:1-2
Reflect: Draw a tree with the Spirit as the trunk. List or draw the "fruit" of the Spirit.
How can you stay connected to the Spirit?

List some of the "fruits" you'd like to see in yourself, as well as the ones you see already. Take a minute to invite God to prune you so you can bear more fruit.

Week Six: Day Two

Read & Repeat: "But the fruit of the Spirit is love, joy, peace, patience, kindness, goodness, faithfulness, gentleness, self-control; against such things there is no law" (Galatians 5:22-23).
Key Word: Joy
Look Up: John 16:16-24 and 1 Peter 1:8-9
Reflect: What do you learn from the verses about God-given joy? How can true joy give you freedom and courage?

In what areas of life do you experience joy? Pray that God will help you manifest joy if you aren't feeling it, and ask for more if you are!

What is one practical way you can share your joy today?

Week Six: Day Three

Read & Repeat: "But the fruit of the Spirit is love, joy, peace, patience, kindness, goodness, faithfulness, gentleness, self-control; against such things there is no law" (Galatians 5:22-23).
Key Phrase: No Law
Look Up: Matthew 6:1-4, Matthew 6:19-21, and Matthew 6:24-34
Reflect: List the "do nots" in these sections of Matthew 6? What fears motivate these behaviors?

What wisdom does Jesus give for avoiding these temptations? How can God's ways enable us to experience freedom, courage, and peace?

What is one practical application Matthew 6 that can take you beyond your current level of courage and strength?

Week Six: Day Four

Read & Repeat: "And those who belong to Christ Jesus have crucified the flesh with its passions and desires" (Galatians 5:24).

Word: Crucified

Look Up: Galatians 6:14

Reflect: What does it mean to crucify the flesh?

In what areas of your life do you need live in the truth that you have been crucified with Christ? What are some practical ways to do this?

What is one thing you can do today stand firm and live for Christ?

Week Six, Day Five

Read & Repeat: If we live by the Spirit, let us also keep in step with the Spirit. Let us not become conceited, provoking one another, envying one another (Galatians 5:25-26).
Key Word: Become
Look Up: Ephesians 4:20-24, Colossians 2:6-7
Reflect: The word *become* also means to grow, happen, come about...what a fitting word to end on! How can keeping in step with the Spirit help you become strong and brave?

Make a list of behaviors/attitudes you need to take off and behaviors/attitudes you need to put on. Pray for the Spirit to work the good fruit of transformation and growth into your life.

What does it mean to live your life in Jesus, rooted and built up in him?

In what ways has God made you brave?

Resources

How to Read the Bible for Personal Study - Appendix A

Let the word of Christ dwell in you richly, teaching and admonishing one another in all wisdom... (Colossians 3:16a)

Studying the Bible for personal use is life-changing. When we are lifelong learners, we are transformed by what we learn as we read God's word. We can study the Bible in a group or alone in our quarters. We study the Bible to seek answers, gain guidance, avoid wrong teaching, and to know God. Reading the Bible increases our spiritual awareness.

Our approach to the Bible matters:

- **Approach the Bible in prayer.** Ask the Holy Spirit to use God's Word to transform you.
- **Approach the Bible with expectancy.** Expect to encounter God in his living Word.
- **Approach the Bible carefully.** Read verses in context, asking who, what, and why.
- **Approach the Bible thoughtfully.** Reflect on your reading by writing in a journal.

Where to Start: If you're not using a study guide like this one, starting with the New Testament can be helpful. Afterwards, read the Old Testament to get a bigger picture. Try reading Bible books from the beginning—even just a chapter at a time—for context. As you read, ask yourself these basic questions:

- What do I learn about God?
- How should I respond?

When to Read the Bible: You can read the Bible anytime. Many people like to read the Bible first thing in the morning to start the day focusing on God. You don't have to read the Bible just once a day either. Anytime you have a few moments for reflection and meditation, the Bible is great inspiration, especially Psalms and Proverbs. Lighter days and weekends can be good times for extended study or longer readings.

Study Aids: Many good "study" Bibles have comments and explanations. Consider reading the Scripture first before turning to the notes. This method allows you to discern the truth firsthand. A good study Bible gives some background on each book, explaining who wrote it, when, and why. If you have questions or concerns, find a solid Bible teacher, chaplain or Christian friend to help you. The Lord has gifted teachers who understand and obey the truth. A good teacher helps us learn the right way to keep in step.

Bottom Line: Approach the Bible prayerfully and humbly for a deeper understanding. Study the verses in context and seek explanations from mature, seasoned Christians.

How to Memorize Scripture - Appendix B

I have stored up your word in my heart... (Psalm 119:11a)

God's Word is foundational to our spiritual maturity.

Storing God's Word in our heart means we have the truth whenever and wherever we need it. We do this by memorizing key and essential verses. Memorization allows Scripture to "take root."

Our generation has more information at our fingertips than ever. Our smartphones, iPads and personal computers are readily available. Technically, we don't have to memorize anything. Even the latest SOP (Standard Operating Procedure) for the unit is available at our fingertips.

Still, memorizing information, especially Holy Scripture, is essential. Smartphones break and iPads lose energy. We must remember important information. A pilot can't forever fly on autopilot. I understand it's not easy. Our memory muscles need development. The more we use our memory muscle, the stronger we get.

Tips for Memorizing Scripture:

- Find a quiet place, free from distractions
- Read the verse(s) at least three times: first for the eyes, second for the mind, third for the heart
- Say the verse out loud, speaking with inflection
- Write it down. Carry it with you and refer to it during down times (in line, etc.)
- Read the passage at night before lights out. You will be amazed what your mind does while you are sleeping! You may awake with the words on your tongue.

As we know in the military, memorization can be a little frustrating at first. But the rewards are remarkable. Take your time. Remember how hard it was to memorize everyone's rank? Now you can recall ranks without a second thought.

Memorizing helps us capture each word and remember it in the future. Engaging with the verse makes memorization easier. Other methods of memorization, such as using music, might help you. Try posting sticky notes in your cover or on the edge of a mirror. Use hand signals or, if you're able, translate the verse into a different language. Repetition is important.

The goal is to let God's Word get deep into the recesses of your heart. Having a memorized verse spring up at just the right moment is encouraging and life-changing!

How to Pray - Appendix C

And he (Jesus) told them a parable to the effect that they ought always to pray and not lose heart. (Luke 18:1)

When we pray, we reach out to God. As simple as a conversation, prayer is both spiritual communion and communication with God. Reverent and sincere, prayer is not some magical formula to get the right results. God is not a magician; he is our heavenly father. Prayer is a conversational relationship, for God desires real and personal communication with us. He's more interested in what concerns us than how we pray.

In Matthew 6:9-13—called the Lord's Prayer—Jesus taught his disciples to pray. Many people use this as a pattern for prayer, and others use it as a daily prayer. Some even do both.

> *Pray then like this: "Our Father in heaven, hallowed be your name. Your kingdom come, your will be done, on earth as it is in heaven. Give us this day our daily bread, and forgive us our debts, as we also have forgiven our debtors. And lead us not into temptation, but deliver us from evil.* (Matthew 6:9-13)

The book of Psalms is full of beautiful prayers. We can pray these back to God, or we can speak to him and praise him freely and personally. Though we can (and should) pray anywhere, Jesus often took extended periods of time and went to solitary places to pray. What should we pray about? Philippians gives us some clues:

> *The Lord is at hand; do not be anxious about anything, but in everything by prayer and supplication with thanksgiving let your requests be made known to God. And the peace of God which surpasses all understanding will guard your hearts and minds in Christ Jesus.* (Philippians 4:5b-7)

When you pray, remember these truths:

- **Draw near to God and he will draw near to you** (James 4:8). Prayer is personal.
- **Pray about everything** (Philippians 4:6). There are no secrets with the all-knowing God.
- **Pray with confidence** (Psalm 62:8). God is not judging the delivery of your prayers.
- **Pray with thankfulness** (Colossians 4:2). Gratitude is one of God's means to guard our hearts.

> "Thus says the Lord who made the earth, the Lord who formed it to establish it—the Lord is his name: Call to me and I will answer you, and will tell you great and hidden things that you have not known. (Jeremiah 33:2-3)

> *"Sirs, what must I do to be saved?" And they said, "Believe in the Lord Jesus, and you will be saved..." And he rejoiced along with his entire household that he had believed in God.* (Acts 16:29-30 & 34)

What does it mean to be a Christian? It means believing in the Lord Jesus for salvation. Many times in the Bible we see the phrase "My Lord and My God." Believing Christ is God is an intellectual belief. Giving him Lordship of your life implies following his leadership--learning his ways and walking in them.

A Christian is a Christ-follower or a disciple. Being a Christian is much like being a military service member in that it requires commitment, faith, and trust. Being a Christian means bearing Christ's name and surrendering to His leadership, sometimes at great personal cost. Our choice to become a service member is only for a short time, but our commitment to Christ lasts a lifetime and beyond.

Christianity is more than a religion. It's a relationship with Christ.

If the idea of being a Christian is new to you, consider the following truths from the Bible:

- **John 14:6** *Jesus said to him, "I am the way, and the truth, and the life. No one comes to the Father except through me."*
- **John 3:16** *"For God so loved the world, that he gave his only Son, that whoever believes in him should not perish but have eternal life."*
- **1 Peter 3:18** *For Christ also suffered once for sins, the righteous for the unrighteous, that he might bring us to God, being put to death in the flesh but made alive in the spirit.*
- **1 John 1:9** *If we confess our sins, he is faithful and just to forgive us our sins and to cleanse us from all unrighteousness.*

Are You Ready?

It simply takes a sincere prayer to be saved.

Lord Jesus, I know I have sinned against you. I come to you today with a repentant heart asking you to forgive my sin. I believe You are the Son of God. You came to earth and chose to die on the cross for me, and then rose again so that I could have eternal life. Beginning today, I surrender my life to you. In the holy name of Jesus, amen.

Facilitator's Guide - Appendix E

But he answered, "It is written, 'Man shall not live by bread alone,
but by every word that comes from the mouth of God.'" (Matthew 4:4)

How to Use this Bible Study

This six-week study can be used individually or as a group. Each week includes:

- A main lesson plus five days of homework geared toward self-discovery
- "Let's Review" questions/journal prompts to aid comprehension and understanding
- "Let's Reflect" questions/journal prompts for personal application and transformation
- "Let's Pray" prompts to encourage us to talk with God about what we learn
- "Let's Play" ideas to reinforce the lesson in fun and meaningful ways
- A weekly memory passage as part of the homework to retain all of Galatians 5

For Individual Use

- Day 1: Read the lesson and reflect on the journal prompts
- Days 2-5: Daily homework includes memory work, word definitions, and journaling

For Group Use

- Begin your gathering with prayer, asking God to guide the discussion.
- The lesson is numbered 1-7 to lead the group through seven different activities including warm up question, reading through Galatians 5 aloud, reading and discussing the lesson (either section-by-section or as a whole), review questions, reflection questions, a prayer prompt, and a weekly activity.
- Facilitator can decide whether to discuss last week's homework (a great motivator to get it done) or simply to focus on the current week's lesson.
- Take time to discuss what the memory verse reveals about God.
- Close in prayer.

Facilitator Helps

- First, **introduce the big idea**--the chapter title or theme
- Second, **resist the temptation to do all the talking.** Self-discovery is important.
- Third, **consider how the weekly memory verse supports the big idea**. Encourage participants in Bible memory. Model this by doing memory work yourself.
- Fourth, **share prayer requests if appropriate** for your group dynamics.
- Finally, **be in prayer for your participants** during the week. Encourage them in faith!

About Planting Roots

Military women, both those in uniform and those that are not, desire connection, stability, hope, and joy. Dealing with multiple moves, frequent deployments, and questions regarding careers, we still must continue to build marriages, raise children, develop relationships, and manage careers. Usually far from family, these challenges can seem insurmountable to accomplish on our own and finding what we need almost impossible.

As military women ourselves, we have walked familiar roads and searched for the same things. What we have come to know and understand is that we do not conquer these obstacles or find the answers on our own. Our only hope for these things is Jesus.

Beginning in January 2014, we began to put together an organization to meet these very needs. These eleven military women launched just such a thing called *Planting Roots* in October 2014.

Planting Roots has a vision to impact military women with the Gospel of Jesus Christ for victorious living. In order to fulfill this vision, our goal is to build a community of military women to provide connection and a biblical foundation where we desire to challenge each other to find stability in Christ and to find His purpose for us in the places we are planted.

In a nutshell, our mission is to encourage military women to grow in their faith. Some of the ways we do this are by building and fostering a community of military women through Christ-centered live events, engaging media channels, and our interactive website where we share our stories and conduct online Bible studies. We strive to reach women with the Gospel and to encourage believers to dig deeply, living out our faith in the place we are planted. We pray that through this effort military women will find the connection, stability, strength, and purpose in our personal lives, in turn building our marriages, families, and communities. Our foundation is in Scripture.

Join us online at www.plantingroots.net, on Facebook and Instagram. We'd love to meet you at one of our live conference. See our website for conference schedule and details.

They will be like a tree planted by the water that sends out its roots by the stream. It does not fear when heat comes; its leaves are always green. It has no worries in a year of drought and never fails to bear fruit.

(Jeremiah 17:8 NIV)

Meet the Author

Andrea Plotner is wife to Todd, and mother to three hungry boys (and twelve exotic pets). A former Army spouse, Andrea has been involved in military women's ministry for 22 years where the rubber meets the road in the form of frequent moves, deployments, and raw difficulties yet where the hope of Christ is real and ready, as it is for all in need (and we're all needy when it comes to God's grace).

Meeting Christ first at a Billy Graham crusade and then through the ministry of Young Life, Andrea has had an insatiable thirst for God's Word since age 16. This thirst prompted studies at Point Loma Nazarene University (BA) and then American University (MA), both of which led to extensive work with churches, parachurches, and non-profit organizations. Andrea is the most recent past-president of PWOC International, and is in her sweet spot when teaching and developing curriculum.

Andrea and her family are grateful to live in Idaho where Andrea coordinates Women's Ministries for her local church, as well as doing a hodge-podge of other things like teaching water aerobics and Pilates classes.

Author of Outrageous Olives and Discipleship 101, Andrea is thrilled help women become grounded in God's Word – our truest source of hope, identity, and strength.

Meet the Editor

Ginger Harrington is the **Publishing Coordinator** for *Planting Roots* and the author of *Holy in the Moment: Simple Ways to Love God and Enjoy Your Life.* An award-winning blogger and engaging speaker for military and civilian audiences, Ginger writes at *GingerHarrington.com* and *PlantingRoots.net.* A contributor for **Heart Renovation** and **Breaking the Chains,** Ginger has also edited and compiled *Free to Be Brave: Moments with God for Military Life.* Ginger and her retired Marine husband have been married for 28 years and have three young adult children. Visit Ginger's website or connect with her on Instagram *@GingerHarrington.*

Editorial Contributors

Liz Giertz is a **staff writer** for *Planting Roots* and an Army Veteran who traded her combat boots for a pink ID Card and a craft apron. She, her husband, their two boisterous boys, and one crazy shelter pup call the hills of West Virginia home, at least until her Soldier retires from active duty. She is passionate about gathering women around her craft table and encouraging them with God's Word. She also writes at lizgiertz.com and has published a pair of workbooks aimed at helping military couples reconnect after deployment, *Marriage Maintenance: Tune Up After Time Apart for Him* and *For Her.*

Melissa Hicks**,** an **editor** for *Planting Roots*, is an Army brat turned Army wife. She has been married 12 years with two sweet children and a snuggly hound named Felix. In between PCS moves, she loves to write, spend time at the beach, and connect with friends new and old around the globe.

Adrienne Schenck is an **editor** for *Planting Roots* and is currently working on her fiction novel. She dabbles occasionally at *adrienneschenck.com* and *plantingroots.net*. She grew up an army brat and then married a soldier. They have three young kids and are in the process to adopt a fourth. Visit Adrienne's website or connect with her on Instagram *@adrienneschenck*.

Design Contributor

Rachelle Whitfield is the **Marketing Coordinator** for *Planting Roots*. She is a veteran, Army wife and mom of four boys, two with four paws. She has been a financial counselor in the military community for over ten years and a residential planner for nearly 20 years. She is passionate about helping military families create a lifestyle full of "*ABUNDANCE.*" Connect with her on Instagram @rachellesamone.

Made in the USA
Middletown, DE
05 February 2019